God's Got Me

Finding Joy in Adversity

By Eugenia J. S. Cawley

Copyright © 2025 by Eugenia J. S. Cawley
Published by Building Wealth Four Generations INC d/b/a
The 1 and Only
All rights reserved.

No part of this book may be reproduced, transmitted, or used in any form or by any means—electronic, mechanical, photocopying, recording, or otherwise—without prior written permission from the publisher, except in the case of brief quotations used in critical reviews or articles.

Scripture quotations are taken from the Holy Bible, New International Version® (NIV®). Copyright ©1973, 1978, 1984, 2011 by Biblica, Inc.™ Used by permission. All rights reserved worldwide.

ISBN: 979-8-89741-010-1

For permission requests, please contact:
The 1 and Only
4500 Forbes Boulevard, STE 200
Lanham, MD 20706
info@the1andonlypublishing.com
www.the1andonlypublishing.com

Dedication

To my younger self-
the girl who cried in silence, prayed with hope, and kept going even when she felt unseen
this is the reminder you needed: God's got you.

And to every woman who picks up this book,
whether you are healing, hoping, wandering, or just holding on
I dedicate these pages to you.

May you find inspiration to draw closer to God,
to make space for Him in your life,
and to embrace a true and lasting relationship with Him.

Most importantly, remember this:
God's Got You—today and always.

Table of Contents

Foreword — 6
Introduction: The Reason I Write — 8

Section 1: Overcoming Emotional and Mental Struggles — 12

Chapter 1: Rediscovering Love — 13
Healing from Feeling Unloved

Chapter 2: Embracing Worth — 19
Conquering Feelings of Insignificance

Chapter 3: Finding Security — 25
Overcoming the Fear of Feeling Unsafe

Chapter 4: Recognizing Care — 31
Transforming the Sense of Being Uncared For

Chapter 5: Belonging Again — 37
Healing from Feeling Othered

Section 2: Navigating Personal Challenges with Faith — 42

Chapter 6: Finding Joy in the Valley — 43
Embracing God's Peace Amid Hardship

Chapter 7: Wrestling with Myself — 49
Inner Struggles and Spiritual Growth

Chapter 8: Wrestling with Others — 55
Cultivating Peace and Understanding in Relationships

Section 3: Empowerment and Resilience — 62

Chapter 9: Self-Advocacy — 63
Becoming Your Own Best Advocate

Chapter 10: Voices of Strength — 69
Knowing and Believing in Your Worth

Chapter 11: Joy in Adversity — 75
Discovering Happiness Even When It's Hard

Chapter Notes and Scripture References — 80

Foreword

When Eugenia first shared the early drafts of what would become "God's Got Me" with me, I knew I was witnessing something extraordinary. Not just because of the powerful narrative that was unfolding on the page, but because of the courage it took for her to put these deeply personal experiences into words.

As a book coach and author, I've had the privilege of working with many writers, each with their unique voice and story. Yet there was something about Eugenia's journey that resonated with particular depth and authenticity. Her willingness to excavate painful memories, to examine the places where she felt invisible, unloved, and unseen, and to reveal how God's presence transformed those experiences---this is the heart of what makes "God's Got Me" not just a memoir, but a testimony.

Maya Angelou wrote, "I come as one, but I stand as ten thousand," and Eugenia embodies this truth beautifully. Her personal story speaks to the universal experiences of seeking worth, belonging, and healing. In sharing her journey from silence to self-advocacy, from pain to purpose, she offers readers not just inspiration but an invitation---to recognize their worth, to find God's presence in their darkest valleys, and to discover joy even in adversity.

What strikes me most about Eugenia's writing is her unflinching honesty paired with profound compassion---both for herself and for others who may be walking similar paths. She doesn't offer platitudes or easy answers. Instead, she shares how faith anchored her through seasons of doubt, how Scripture became a lifeline when human connection failed, and how God's love proved constant even when everything else seemed uncertain.

As you turn these pages, I encourage you to read not just with your mind but with your heart. Allow Eugenia's words to create space for your reflection, for your journey toward healing and wholeness. Whether you're wrestling with feelings of being unloved, struggling to find security, or searching for joy amid hardship, "God's Got Me" reminds us that we are never truly alone.

It has been my honor to walk alongside Eugenia as this book took shape, to witness her transform painful memories into powerful messages of hope and redemption. Her voice---once silenced by cultural expectations and personal doubts---now rings clear and true, reminding us that our stories matter, that our pain has purpose, and that God's love can transform our deepest wounds into sources of strength.

May this book be a blessing to you, just as Eugenia's friendship and faith have been to me.

With deep respect and admiration,

Jori O'Neale
2x Best-Selling Author & Book Coach

Introduction: The Reason I Write

In writing this book, I am reminded of a quote by the late poet and activist Maya Angelou: "I come as one, but I stand as ten thousand." Every time I hear those words, they remind me that even when I feel alone, I am not. My journey---the heartaches, the triumphs, the silent moments---is not mine alone. It is connected to countless others, to women and men who have walked similar paths, felt similar pains, and wrestled with similar doubts. None of us walks through this life in isolation, even when it feels like we do.

There have been so many times when I felt invisible. I've wondered if my voice mattered at all, or if the weight of my experiences had any purpose. I've sat with these questions, doubting whether I could---or even should---share my story. Why write this book? Why share so much of myself? Will it even make a difference? These thoughts have often stopped me in my tracks. But in those moments of doubt, God speaks. He reminds me, in the quiet of my heart, through scripture and prayer, that my story is not just for me. It's for someone else---someone who needs to hear it, someone who needs to know they are not alone.

Maya Angelou's words, "I come as one, but I stand as ten thousand," resonate deeply with me because they embody the power of connection. When I tell my story, I'm not just speaking for myself; I'm speaking for the many women who have felt silenced, unseen, or unheard. I write this book for them---for the ones who are carrying their pain quietly, unsure if anyone would care to listen if they spoke up. I want this book to say to them, "I hear you. I see you. You are not alone."

This book is my way of breaking the silence---not just my silence, but the silence so many of us have carried for too long. I've spent years keeping my struggles to myself, thinking that my story wasn't worth telling or no one would care. But as I've grown in my faith and listened to others, I've realized how much power there is in being vulnerable. There's power in saying, "This is my truth. This is what I've been through." There's power in showing up, just as you are, and allowing others to see the messiness, the imperfections, the pain---and the beauty that comes from it all.

None of this has been easy. There were times when I questioned God's plan for my life, times when I felt forgotten, rejected, and completely alone. I cried out to Him, asking Why? Why is this happening? Why am I going through this? For years, I struggled to grasp the answers. But now, looking back, I can see how God was with me every step of the way. He never left me, not even in my darkest moments. He was there, carrying me, shaping me, preparing me for this purpose.

As women, we carry so much---so many joys, so many sorrows, so many stories waiting to be told. And yet, so often, we are silenced. We are told to keep quiet, to carry our burdens alone, to pretend everything is fine even when it's not. But I've learned that silence doesn't heal---it isolates. And that's why I can't stay silent anymore. I can't keep quiet when I know there are women who feel like their voices don't matter. Because they do. You do. Your story matters. Your pain matters. And when we share our stories, we create something powerful---a connection that reminds us we're not alone.

Maya Angelou's quote reminds me that when we speak, we don't speak just for ourselves. We speak for the ten thousand---those who came before us, those who walk alongside us, and those who will come after us. That's why I'm writing this book---not just for myself but for every woman who has ever felt invisible, for every girl who has ever doubted her worth, and for every soul who needs to hear the words, "You are seen. You are loved. You are not alone."

Writing this book is also my way of stepping fully into my truth. One of my favorite mottos is "Be human." To me, that means embracing all of who we are---the pain and the joy, the heartbreak and the healing, the imperfections and the beauty. It means showing up, even when it's hard, and saying, "This is me. This is my journey." Writing this book is my way of doing that---not just for myself but for every woman who needs permission to do the same.

So here I am, sharing my story because it's time. I'm doing this for the women who are still finding their voices, for the girls who are growing up in a world that tries to silence them, and for the generations who will stand on our shoulders. Of this, I am living proof because He held me when I thought I couldn't go on. He saw me when I felt invisible. And because of His love, I can say with confidence: "I come as one, but I stand as ten thousand."

Footnotes

1. Maya Angelou's quote is from her poem Our Grandmothers, which speaks to resilience, strength, and the interconnectedness of all women. It reminds us that our stories don't stand alone---they are part of a larger, collective journey.
2. Silent suffering, especially among women, is common in many communities. Breaking this silence is a powerful act of healing.
3. Vulnerability, as Brené Brown writes in The Gifts of Imperfection, allows for true connection and courage. Sharing our stories is one of the bravest acts we can undertake.
4. The collective power of women's voices has transformed history, from civil rights to community-building. Sharing our stories continues that legacy.
5. Be human emphasizes authenticity and the courage to embrace our imperfections. It's a reminder that we don't have to be perfect to be loved.

Section 1:

Overcoming Emotional and Mental Struggles

"We cannot find peace by avoiding life" - Virginia Woolf

Chapter 1

Rediscovering Love
Healing from Feeling Unloved

The Fragrance of Memory

The smell of incense brings it all back---the Friday nights spent in Mother Mason's home, when her small house became a makeshift church. My great-aunt took me, my cousin, and my younger sister there faithfully, week after week. We'd sit through the prayers, the songs, and the lessons. I remember the way the incense filled every corner of the room, clinging to our clothes and our hair. By the time we left, we were practically drenched in the smell, carrying it home with us like an invisible covering. To me, it felt like God was wrapping us in His presence, even though I didn't fully understand what it meant back then.

At the time, I didn't see that those nights were planting seeds of faith in my life. I only knew that I hated being there---hated the hours we spent praying and singing. But now when I look back, I realize that God was there, even in those moments when I felt most invisible, most unloved. He was with me, covering me like that incense, even when the people around me weren't.

The Ache of Feeling Unloved

Growing up, I longed for love and acceptance from the people who should have shown it most---my family. But instead of hugs and kind words, I felt ignored, like I was an afterthought. The adults in my life, the ones I relied on to guide and care for me, seemed distant, preoccupied, uninterested. Their indifference left a mark on me, one that took years to fade.

I tried to make peace with this difference in my own way. I told myself it didn't matter, that I didn't need them to notice me. But at night, when the house was quiet and everyone else was asleep, the memories would come rushing back. I'd lie in bed, holding my body still, as if that could keep the pain from bubbling up. But it didn't work. The memories played on repeat: the moments when I was overlooked, the harsh comments, the times when I needed help and no one came.

One of the hardest things for me was forgiving them. I prayed about it often, asking God to help me let go of the hurt. But it felt impossible. I couldn't understand how the people who were supposed to love me the most could make me feel so small.

Moments That Stung

The isolation I felt as a child carried over into my teenage years, and showed up in ways I didn't fully understand at the time. I remember the painful acne that broke out on my face during my teens---big, red, angry blemishes that made even smiling hurt. I was embarrassed to show my face, but I didn't know what to do. There were three adult women in the house, but no one ever sat me down to explain how to take care of my skin.

Instead, I tried to fix it on my own. I scrubbed my face raw, desperate to make the blemishes disappear. I even slept with toothpaste smeared across my cheeks because I'd heard somewhere that it could dry out pimples. But nothing worked. And when my aunt asked, "What's that on your face?" it wasn't because she wanted to help. It was to remind me of what I already knew: my face was a mess.

The silence around my body---my skin, my period, my changing self---made me feel like I was walking through life blindfolded. When I got my first period, I didn't know what was happening. No one had prepared me for it. I kept it to myself, hiding my pads and praying no one would notice. It was as if even my body was something to be ashamed of.

The White Skirt Incident

There's one memory that sticks with me more than most. We were living with my grandmother's younger sister in a cramped house, sharing space with her family. Money was tight, and tensions were high. I'd started my period, but because I didn't know how to manage it properly, I made do with what I had. I was wearing a white jean skirt that day---a bold choice, in hindsight---but I thought I'd prepared well enough.

I walked to the shoemaker to get my slippers fixed, confident that I'd covered myself adequately. I sat down on a stool to wait, completely unaware of the stain forming on the back of my skirt. When the shoemaker called me over to pick up my slippers, a woman nearby stopped me. "You're bleeding," she said, pointing at my skirt. I felt my heart drop. My stomach churned with embarrassment. I didn't have a jacket or scarf to cover myself, so I turned my skirt around and used the plastic bag I was carrying to hide the stain. As I hurried home, my mind raced. What if more people had seen me? What if someone recognized me?

When I got home, my grandmother asked why I was crying, but I couldn't bring myself to tell her. Instead, I stripped off the skirt, scrubbed it clean, and hung it to dry. I told myself, "It's okay. It'll be okay." But it wasn't. I felt humiliated, ashamed, and utterly alone. That incident became a symbol of how unsupported I felt---even my most basic needs were mine to figure out on my own.

Turning to God

In the midst of all this pain, there was one constant: God. Even when I didn't feel His presence, He was there, guiding me, comforting me in ways I didn't always recognize. My faith became my anchor, the thing that kept me grounded when everything else felt chaotic.

Forgiveness was one of the hardest lessons I had to learn. I struggled to forgive the people who had hurt me, but I also realized I needed to forgive myself. I had to let go of the anger I felt toward my younger self---the girl who had tried so hard to be perfect, to be good enough for people who never even noticed her. Through prayer and reflection, I began to see myself the way God sees me: not as a broken, rejected person but as someone fearfully and wonderfully made.

One moment that stands out is a conversation I had with my stepmother. My sister and I confronted her about our father's favoritism, pouring out years of frustration. I learned later that my father overheard the conversation and cried. That small moment felt like a breakthrough---not just for him, but for me. It reminded me that healing doesn't always come in the ways we expect.

The more I leaned on God, the more I realized that His love was the only love I truly needed. Verses such as Jeremiah 31:3---"I have loved you with an everlasting love; I have drawn you with loving-kindness" (NIV)---became my lifelines, reminders that I was never alone.

Rediscovering Love

Looking back, I see how those early experiences shaped me. They taught me resilience, but more importantly, they showed me the depth of God's love. Even when I felt invisible, God saw me. Even when I felt unloved, He called me His own.

Forgiveness didn't come easily, but it came. And with it came freedom---freedom from the anger and bitterness that had weighed me down for so long. At the time, I didn't see that those Friday nights in Mother Mason's home were planting seeds of faith in my life. I only knew that I hated being there---hated the hours we spent praying and singing. But now when I look back, I realize that God was there, even in those moments when I felt most invisible, most unloved. He was with me, covering me like that incense, even when the people around me weren't. Sometimes, the love we need most is the love we find in God.

Scriptures and Reflection Questions

Scriptures:

1. Psalm 34:18: "The Lord is close to the brokenhearted and saves those who are crushed in spirit." (NIV)
2. Romans 8:38-39: "For I am convinced that neither death nor life, neither angels nor demons, neither the present nor the future, nor any powers, neither height nor depth, nor anything else in all creation, will be able to separate us from the love of God that is in Christ Jesus our Lord." (NIV)

Reflection Questions:

1. Have you ever felt unloved or invisible? How did it affect your relationship with others and with God?
2. What steps can you take to forgive those who have hurt you, and how can you begin forgiving yourself?
3. In what ways has God shown you love, even in your most difficult moments?

Call to Action

1. **Journal Your Journey:** Write about a time when you felt unseen or unsupported. Reflect on how that experience shaped you and what God might be teaching you through it.
2. **Pray for Healing:** Bring your pain to God in prayer; ask Him to help you forgive and heal.
3. **Embrace Scripture:** Meditate on verses such as Jeremiah 31:3, reminding yourself daily of God's love and faithfulness.

Chapter 2

Embracing Worth
Conquering Feelings of Insignificance

"The Lord is close to the brokenhearted and saves those who are crushed in spirit." ---Psalm 34:18 (NIV)

"For you created my inmost being; you knit me together in my mother's womb. I praise you because I am fearfully and wonderfully made; your works are wonderful, I know that full well." ---Psalm 139:13-14 (NIV)

Feeling Unseen and Overlooked

There are moments in life that leave invisible marks on our hearts---marks we carry long after the moments have passed. For me, one of those marks was the feeling of insignificance; it was a quiet belief that I wasn't seen or valued the way I longed to be. It didn't start all at once, but it took root over time; in the small, silent ways my needs went unnoticed.

Take my childhood for example. My aunt, my dad's younger sister, was a traveling nurse. She dedicated her life to helping others, often traveling across the country to teach new mothers how to care for their babies. Because of her, my cousins, my younger sister, and I received every vaccine available to us. You'd think this would be comforting, but for me, it wasn't. I dreaded those shots more than anything. Unlike my younger sister and cousins, who seemed to handle the vaccines without much trouble, I was left shaken every time. This bred a fear of needles that stayed with me, and even to this day, I only get shots when it is an absolute must.

But it wasn't just the vaccines. Growing up, I was often sickly.

Summers, which should have been filled with joy and freedom, became a season of struggle. Year after year, just as school let out, I would fall ill. My birthday, a time meant for celebration, was often spent in bed. Even with all the vaccines my aunt ensured we received, nothing could prevent the fevers, aches, and fatigue that plagued me. And no one ever asked why.

What hurt even more were the things no one noticed. For years, I endured heavy menstrual cycles that left me bedridden with unbearable cramps, bloating, and nausea. The pain was so intense that I couldn't walk, eat, or sleep. But no one in my family---neither the women on my mother's side nor those on my father's side---seemed to see what I was going through. I didn't talk about it, and they didn't ask. I learned to suffer in silence, convincing myself that this was just the way life was.

A Breaking Point

By the time I reached my fourth year in college, I thought I had learned to manage the pain. I was pursuing both my bachelor's and master's degrees, balancing a demanding schedule with high expectations. But one night, everything came crashing down. I was struck with abdominal pain of a force I had never felt before. It was unbearable---I couldn't sleep, couldn't eat, and couldn't even stand. It felt as though my body was turning against me.

My mother, the only person home at the time, saw my condition and immediately called a cab to take me to Elmhurst Hospital. We sat in the emergency room for what felt like an eternity, waiting for answers. When I was finally seen by a doctor, they began a series of tests. The poking, prodding, and endless questions only added to my frustration. How could I explain a pain that felt as if it were everywhere and nowhere all at once?

After hours of waiting, the tests came back. The diagnosis: endometriosis. The doctors explained that the condition was causing the lining of my uterus to grow outside its boundaries, leading to the excruciating pain I had been experiencing for years. They recommended surgery to manage the condition. But with exams just around the corner, I couldn't afford the recovery time. Instead, I opted for a laparoscopy, a less invasive procedure that allowed me to return to school the next day.

At the time, I thought the problem was solved. The pain had lessened, and I convinced myself it was over. I didn't ask questions about the diagnosis or its long-term implications. I didn't research treatments or seek additional support. I simply moved on, ignoring the thorn in my flesh that would continue to haunt me for years to come.

Trusting God Amid the Pain

For years, I believed that modern medicine would give me the answers I needed. Every time I visited a doctor, I prayed silently, God, please let them tell me I'm healed. Let this be the visit where everything changes. I clung to my faith, believing that the same God who healed the sick and raised the dead could do the same for me.

But each visit brought the same diagnosis---or worse. The doctors informed me that the endometrial tissue was not shrinking but growing. They prescribed birth control pills to help manage the symptoms. For a time, I thought this was the breakthrough for which I had been praying. The pills reduced the intensity of my cycles and offered some relief, but the underlying condition remained. Eventually, I underwent two more laparoscopies, each one revealing how persistent the endometriosis had become. The tissue had grown to the size of golf balls, and the doctors were running out of options.

I was placed on Depo-Provera, a birth control shot administered every three months. Without a car, I relied on trains and buses to get to my appointments at JFK Medical. It was exhausting, but I kept going, holding onto the belief that God had placed these doctors in my life for a reason. I told myself that this was His way of guiding me toward healing.

Through it all, I found solace in the story of the woman in the Bible who had been bleeding for 12 years. She believed that if she could just touch the hem of Jesus's garment, she would be healed. Her faith inspired me. I wasn't bleeding for 18 years, but I felt her desperation. I believed that if I had enough faith, God would heal me too.

Embracing My Worth

Looking back, I see now that my worth was never tied to my health---or lack of it. For years, I believed that being "fixed" would make me whole. I thought that if I could just solve this one problem, everything else would fall into place. But God had a different plan. He showed me that my worth wasn't based on my physical condition or my ability to be "perfect." My worth was, and always has been, rooted in Him.

Reflection Questions

1. Reflect on a time when you felt unseen or overlooked. How did it affect your sense of worth?
2. What are the hidden wounds from your past that you've been afraid to confront? How might God be calling you to heal from them?
3. How has God reminded you of your worth during times when you felt insignificant?

Closing Scripture:

"Are not two sparrows sold for a penny? Yet not one of them will fall to the ground apart from the will of your Father. And even the very hairs of your head are all numbered. So don't be afraid; you are worth more than many sparrows." ---*Matthew 10:29-31 (NIV)*

Chapter 3

Finding Security
Overcoming the Fear of Feeling Unsafe

"Heal me, O Lord, and I will be healed; save me and I will be saved, for you are the one I praise." ---*Jeremiah 17:14 (NIV)*

"God is our refuge and strength, an ever-present help in trouble." ---*Psalm 46:1 (NIV)*

"The name of the Lord is a strong tower; the righteous run to it and are safe." ---*Proverbs 18:10 (NIV)*

The Fear of Feeling Unsafe

Fear is a shadow that creeps in quietly and takes hold of our heart before we even realize it's there. It whispers lies that grow louder with every passing moment: You're not safe. You're not protected. You're on your own. For me, this shadow began casting itself early in life, in spaces where I should have felt secure but didn't. Over time, those moments planted seeds of insecurity that shaped how I viewed myself and the world around me.

One memory stands out as particularly pivotal. I was a young girl hanging clothes outside, a routine chore on an otherwise ordinary day. The sun was warm against my skin, the air was calm, and I was lost in the rhythm of pinning damp clothes to the line. But then, I felt it---a prickling at the back of my neck, like the faint brush of unseen fingers. I turned, and that's when I saw him.

An older man stood a short distance away, watching me. His eyes weren't wandering or distracted; they were fixed on me, following my every move. His gaze carried a weight that made my stomach churn and my skin crawl. I tried to focus on my task, pretending not to notice, but the unease was impossible to shake. My hands trembled as I hurried to finish, each clothespin slipping from my fingers. As soon as I could, I rushed back inside, closing the door behind me and leaning against it as if the barrier could protect me from the weight of his eyes.

Even though I was safe in my home, the fear lingered. That moment left an imprint on me, not just because of what happened but because of what it revealed: that I could feel unsafe even in my own space. It wasn't just about the man or his stare. It was about the realization that I was vulnerable, that protection wasn't guaranteed, and that I would have to fend for myself in ways I didn't yet understand.

The Lingering Effects of Fear

Fear doesn't always announce itself loudly. Sometimes, it creeps in quietly, slowly embedding itself in the fabric of our lives until it feels normal. After that day, I became hyper-aware of my surroundings, constantly on guard. I started anticipating threats where there might not have been any, my mind racing with "what ifs" that painted every situation in shades of danger.

But it wasn't just external fears that haunted me. Growing up, there were other moments---smaller, quieter ones---that reinforced my sense of vulnerability. One of these was the silence surrounding anything related to my body. When I got my first period, I had no idea what to do. No one had prepared me for that moment. The blood, the cramps, the discomfort---it all felt overwhelming, like I had crossed a threshold for which I wasn't ready.

More than the physical pain, what hurt the most was the shame that seemed to come with it. It was as though I had done something wrong simply by becoming a woman. The silence around menstruation made it feel like a secret I had to keep, something to be hidden. I would crumple makeshift pads into tiny balls, burying them deep in the trash. I scrubbed stains out of my clothes in secret, my heart pounding at the thought of someone finding out. The fear of being exposed, of being seen in a way I wasn't ready for, consumed me.

I didn't talk about it, and no one brought it up. That silence only made the fear grow. It whispered lies that something about me was shameful, that I had to hide parts of myself to be accepted. It made me feel small, unseen, and alone.

Trusting God as My Refuge

Over time, I began to understand that I couldn't navigate these fears alone. I had spent years trying to control my environment, to anticipate every potential threat, to shield myself from anything that might make me feel exposed or vulnerable. But no amount of hyper-awareness could give me the security I craved. True safety wasn't something I could create on my own; it was something I had to find in God.

The first step was prayer. I started asking God to be my protector, my refuge, my shield. At first, it was difficult to let go of control. I wanted immediate solutions, tangible evidence that I was safe. But God's protection doesn't always look the way we expect, and it doesn't always come on our timeline. Slowly, as I prayed, I began to feel a shift. The fear that had once felt so overwhelming started to loosen its grip.

I also took practical steps to create a sense of safety for myself. I learned to trust my instincts, to listen to the quiet nudges that told me when a situation didn't feel right. I began surrounding myself with people who respected my boundaries and made me feel secure. And in the moments when I couldn't control my environment, I leaned into the promise that God was with me, even when I felt most vulnerable.

When it came to the shame I carried about my body, the journey was similar. I started by educating myself---reading, asking questions, and opening up to trusted women in my life. Through prayer,

I asked God to help me see my body as He does: a creation fearfully and wonderfully made (Psalm 139:14). Slowly, the shame began to lift. I realized that the secrecy and silence surrounding menstruation weren't mine to carry---they were part of a culture that taught me to hide. By breaking that silence, I reclaimed my sense of worth and security.

Confidence in God's Protection

The goal wasn't to eliminate fear entirely. Fear can serve as a signal, a reminder to be cautious. But I didn't want fear to control me. I wanted to acknowledge it without letting it dictate my actions. Most importantly, I wanted to trust in God's protection more than fear the threats around me.

Looking back, I see how God was present in every moment, even when I didn't realize it. His protection wasn't always about removing the threat but about giving me the strength to face it. He was my refuge, my strength, my ever-present help in trouble (Psalm 46:1). Knowing this has transformed the way I approach fear. It no longer paralyzes me; instead, it pushes me closer to God, reminding me of His unwavering presence.

Breaking the Silence

Fear thrives in silence. When we keep our struggles to ourselves, when we hide the things that make us feel vulnerable, fear grows stronger. But when we bring those fears into the light---when we name them and share them with God and trusted others---they begin to lose their hold.

Breaking the silence wasn't easy for me. It meant confronting the lies I had believed for so long: that my worth was tied to my ability to protect myself, that my body was something to be ashamed of, that I had to handle everything alone. But each time I opened up, each time I brought my fears to God, I felt a little more free.

Now, I want to be someone who creates safe spaces for others. I want the people in my life to know that they can come to me with their fears, their struggles, their insecurities, and find compassion instead of judgment. And I want to remind them of the truth I've come to know: that no matter how vulnerable we feel, we are never alone. God is our refuge, our strength, our ever-present help.

It is also important to note that the safe places we create don't only need to be associated with struggles or danger; they may also be more nuanced-seemingly insignificant and go overlooked by many.

One memory from my time at Flushing High School drives this point home. After failing to pass the GED exam, I was forced to return to high school, even though I had already graduated back home. I was older than my classmates, and though I excelled academically, I often felt out of place. One day, in French class, a classmate stole my report card. When I confronted her, she confessed that she wanted it because grades like mine would have made her family celebrate her achievements.

Her confession struck a nerve. My family neither celebrated my grades nor any of my accomplishments. My mother would glance at my report card and say, "Good job," but that was it. No hugs. No gifts. No recognition. In that moment, I realized how much I longed for validation---not for what I did, but for who I was.

Today, I make it a point to celebrate others---my friends, my family, their children---because I never want anyone to feel the way I did. And more importantly, I've learned to celebrate myself, not because of what I achieve but because of who God says I am. My classmate had let the fear that came with her family not celebrating her abilities control her and lead her to negative actions. In the same way I had let my fears and insecurities about my body control me for so long. We all have different struggles, but we also all have the same God who is a constant who accepts us just as we are. He has not only created our bodies and our minds but also equipped us with a spirit that is not made to fear. I no longer have a fear of lack of validation because in God I know I'm enough. He celebrates me just as I am.

Reflection Questions

1. Think about a time when you felt unsafe or vulnerable. How did that experience shape your sense of security?
2. What are the areas of your life where fear still has a hold? How might God be calling you to release those fears to Him?
3. How can you create safer environments for yourself and others?

Closing Scriptures:

"Heal me, O Lord, and I will be healed; save me and I will be saved, for you are the one I praise." ---*Jeremiah 17:14 (NIV)*

"The name of the Lord is a strong tower; the righteous run to it and are safe." ---*Proverbs 18:10 (NIV)*

"For God did not give us a spirit of timidity, but a spirit of power, of love and of self-discipline." ---*2 Timothy 1:7 (NIV)*

Chapter 4

*Recognizing Care
Transforming the Sense of
Being Uncared For*

"We are hard pressed on every side, but not crushed; perplexed, but not in despair; persecuted, but not abandoned; struck down, but not destroyed."
---*2 Corinthians 4:8-9 (NIV)*

"Cast all your anxiety on him because he cares for you." ---*1 Peter 5:7 (NIV)*

"Cast your cares on the Lord and he will sustain you; he will never let the righteous fall." ---*Psalm 55:22 (NIV)*

Feeling Uncared For

There's a unique ache that comes from feeling uncared for. It's not always loud or obvious---it doesn't necessarily come with dramatic arguments or public betrayals. Sometimes, it's the quieter moments that hurt the most: the absence of acknowledgment, the lack of a kind word, the feeling that no one notices you at all. For much of my childhood and young adulthood, this was my reality.

I longed for someone to care in a way that made me feel seen and valued. I wanted someone to ask me how I was doing, to truly listen, to show up for me. Instead, I often felt invisible. When I voiced my concerns, they were dismissed, twisted into accusations that left me questioning myself. Was I really wrong? Was I bad? Was I too much? Over time, I stopped speaking up. I convinced myself that my voice didn't matter, that my pain wasn't significant enough for anyone to address.

One of the most vivid examples of this was my relationship with my dad---or, more accurately, the absence of one. Although we lived in the same city, I could count on one hand the number of times I saw him. He was always too busy, too preoccupied with his own life and his sister and her children to make time for my younger sister and me.

Every weekend, we would visit my aunt, bringing food for my dad and grandfather. Yet, every time, it felt as if we were delivering something to people who barely acknowledged our existence. I remember sitting on the veranda, week after week, waiting for him to show up. My heart clung to the hope that this time would be different, that he would come out and spend time with us, that he would choose us. But most of the time, he didn't.

I used to wonder, Doesn't he know we're waiting? Doesn't he realize how much I need him here? The pain of that rejection ran deep, but I buried it. I told myself it didn't matter, but each time we left without seeing him, the void in my heart grew.

The Compounding Pain of Being Overlooked

What made this even harder to bear was knowing that my dad made time for others. He had remarried and taken on the responsibility of caring for his new wife, a new baby boy, and her family. I saw firsthand how he showed up for them---how he poured love, attention, and resources into their lives. It was everything I had longed for but never received. When we visited him and his new family in Maryland, my sister and I would sleep on the floor while his new family lived comfortably. It was a glaring reminder that we weren't his priority.

Why not me? That question haunted me. Why didn't I deserve the same care? I started to believe that there was something fundamentally wrong with me, something that made me unworthy of his love.

Then there was the rumor---a whisper I didn't want to believe-

--that my dad and his sister had an inappropriate relationship, and that my cousin was the product of that relationship. I don't know if it was true, but every time I felt abandoned, it was easy to blame my aunt and cousin. In my mind, they had taken the place in my dad's heart that I so desperately wanted to occupy.

The mix of anger and sadness I carried became a heavy burden. It wasn't just about my dad---it was about what his absence represented. If he, the one person who should have cared most for me, couldn't see my worth, how could I expect anyone else to? That sense of being overlooked spilled over into other areas of my life, shaping how I viewed myself and my relationships with others.

Learning to Recognize God's Care

For years, I tried to make sense of why the people who were supposed to care for me didn't. I wondered what I had done wrong. I thought that if I could just be better---more obedient, more helpful, more loving---then maybe things would change. But no matter how hard I tried, it didn't make a difference. Eventually, I realized that I had to stop chasing after a love that wasn't mine to receive.

In the quiet moments of my pain, God began to show me a different kind of love. While my dad and others had failed to care for me, God had been there all along. His presence was constant, even when I didn't see it. Slowly, I began to understand that my worth wasn't determined by the love or care I did or didn't receive from others. My worth came from being a child of God.

Through prayer, I started asking God to help me let go of the hurt and disappointment that had weighed me down for so long. I asked Him to fill the empty places in my heart, to be the caregiver I had always needed. It wasn't an instant fix, but with time, I felt a change. The more I leaned into God's love, the less power those old wounds had over me.

I also learned to care for myself in ways I had never allowed before. I stopped waiting for others to provide the love and validation

I needed and began nurturing my own soul. I prayed more, journaled my thoughts and feelings, and sought out scriptures that reminded me of God's unwavering care. Passages such as 1 Peter 5:7---"Cast all your anxiety on him because he cares for you" (NIV)---became lifelines, anchoring me in the truth that I was never truly alone.

The Power of Forgiveness

One of the most transformative parts of this journey was learning to forgive my dad. For years, I carried anger and resentment toward him, convinced that his absence was proof that I didn't matter. But as I grew in my faith, I began to see things differently.

Forgiveness didn't mean excusing his actions or pretending they didn't hurt me. It didn't mean that I would ever get the love and care I had wanted from him. What it meant was releasing the hold that pain had on my heart. Holding onto that anger was like drinking poison and expecting it to hurt someone else---it only harmed me. Forgiving him was my way of choosing freedom, of stepping into the fullness of God's love instead of clinging to the scraps of my dad's love.

I also began to see my dad as a person with his own struggles and limitations. I don't know what shaped his choices or why he couldn't be the father I needed. But I do know that his shortcomings don't define my worth. God's care is constant and complete, and that is enough for me.

Finding God's Care in the Quiet

As I reflect on these experiences, I realize how often we overlook the ways God cares for us. We get so caught up in the pain of rejection or neglect that we fail to see the quiet ways He is present. But His care is there---in the moments of peace that come after prayer, in the friends who offer encouragement, in the strength we find to keep going even when the road is hard.

God's care doesn't always look the way we expect. It's not always loud or dramatic. Sometimes, it's as simple as a sunrise after a long night, a reminder that His mercies are new every morning. When I look back now, I can see His fingerprints all over my life, even in the moments when I felt most alone.

Reflection Questions

1. Reflect on a time when you felt uncared for or overlooked. How did that experience shape your sense of worth?
2. Where has God shown His care in your life, even when others failed you?
3. How can you begin to trust in God's constant care, even when you feel forgotten by others?
4. In what ways can you offer care to yourself and others as a reflection of God's love?

Closing Scripture:

"Cast your cares on the Lord and he will sustain you; he will never let the righteous fall." ---*Psalm 55:22 (NIV)*

Chapter 5

Belonging Again
Healing from Feeling Othered

"For we are God's workmanship, created in Christ Jesus to do good works, which God prepared in advance for us to do." ---*Ephesians 2:10 (NIV)*

"Therefore we do not lose heart. Though outwardly we are wasting away, yet inwardly we are being renewed day by day. For our light and momentary troubles are achieving for us an eternal glory that far outweighs them all. So we fix our eyes not on what is seen, but on what is unseen. For what is seen is temporary, but what is unseen is eternal." ---*2 Corinthians 4:16-18 (NIV)*

Feeling Othered

There's anguish that comes with feeling like you don't belong. It's not just about being left out; it's a deeper pain of believing that there's something about you---something unchangeable---that sets you apart from everyone else. This feeling of being "othered" doesn't just isolate you from others; it can make you question your worth altogether.

For me, this ache began in childhood. I was often the one in my family who got sick, no matter the season. My family relied on homemade remedies---steaming herbal teas, pungent oils, and secret combinations of spices---that seemed to work miracles for everyone else. But not for me. My body seemed determined to resist every attempt at healing, and it left me feeling isolated. I didn't know how to explain it to my family, and honestly, I don't think they knew how to respond. Their remedies worked for them, so why didn't they work for me?

I began to feel like an outlier, even within my own home. It wasn't just that I was physically unwell---it was the way my struggles set me apart. It was the unspoken question lingering in my mind: Why can't I just be like everyone else? That question followed me into adolescence and adulthood, showing up in relationships and friendships where I constantly felt like I had to earn my place.

The Search for Belonging

That search for belonging led me to places I should have avoided. One of the most painful examples of this was my relationship with L. Bailey. I was young, inexperienced, and desperate for someone to love me. He saw that desperation and used it to his advantage.

At first, he seemed perfect. He said all the right things, made me feel special, and promised me the affection I had always longed for. But it didn't take long for his true nature to reveal itself. He cheated on me---not once, but repeatedly---with two of my so-called friends, Michelle and Lisa. Both women were beautiful and confident; everything I thought I wasn't.

What hurt most wasn't just the betrayal itself but the confirmation of my deepest fear: that I wasn't enough. I convinced myself that if I just tried harder, if I just loved him more, he would finally choose me. But he didn't. Instead, he spread lies about me throughout our school, tarnishing my reputation and leaving me even more isolated than before.

Ignoring the Red Flags

Looking back, I can see the red flags clearly. But at the time, I was so blinded by my need for validation that I ignored every warning sign. I even brushed off the advice of an older woman who tried to warn me about L. Bailey. She barely knew me, but she saw what I couldn't: that he was using my insecurities to keep me trapped in a toxic cycle.

I didn't want to hear her advice. I thought she didn't understand; she was out of touch with what I was going through. But now, I see her for what she truly was---a vessel for God's wisdom, sent to pull me out of a situation I didn't have the strength to leave on my own.

The moment that finally broke me came when I learned that L. Bailey had gotten Lisa pregnant and pressured her into having an abortion. Even then, I stayed. I told myself that his actions didn't change how much I loved him. I clung to the little bits of attention he gave me, even though deep down, I knew he didn't truly care for me.

The Depth of Desperation

I'll never forget the night I cried out to God in desperation. I was in the shower, tears streaming down my face, when I said, "If I can't have him, then I won't have anything to do with You." Those words still sting when I think about them. I had placed L. Bailey on a pedestal so high that I was willing to turn my back on God for him.

When I confronted L. Bailey about his cheating, his response was cold and unapologetic. "Once I started lying, I couldn't stop," he said, as if that explained everything. That was the moment I finally saw the truth. I was never his priority. I was just someone he used to boost his ego.

The heartbreak was devastating, but even more than that, I was ashamed of how low I had let myself sink. I had given so much of myself to someone who never deserved it, all because I wanted to feel like I belonged.

Finding True Belonging in God

The healing process wasn't easy, but it began when I stopped looking for love and belonging in people who couldn't provide it. I realized that no human being could fill the emptiness inside me---only God could.

Through prayer and reflection, I began to understand that my worth didn't come from the approval or attention of others. My worth came from being a child of God. Verses like Psalm 139:14---"I praise you because I am fearfully and wonderfully made; your works are wonderful, I know that full well" (NIV)---became lifelines for me. They reminded me that my value wasn't dependent on anyone else's validation. God had already declared my worth, and His love for me was unshakable.

I also started to recognize the people God placed in my life who genuinely cared for me. That older woman who warned me about L. Bailey? She was one of the many ways God was trying to guide me, even when I was too blinded by my own desires to see it.

By surrounding myself with people who uplifted me and reflected God's love, I began to heal. I stopped forcing myself into relationships and spaces where I wasn't valued. Instead, I leaned into God's love and the truth of who He created me to be.

Embracing True Belonging

The result of this journey was a profound shift in how I saw myself. I no longer sought my sense of worth in the hands of people who didn't deserve it. I stopped chasing after love that wasn't real and started embracing the love that God had for me all along.

I now see that true belonging doesn't come from fitting in with the world---it comes from being embraced by God. He has shown me time and time again that I was never "othered" in His eyes. I was always part of His plan, always worthy of His love, even when I couldn't see it.

If I could go back, I would tell myself to listen to the wisdom that God places around us. I would tell myself that being loved by someone who doesn't truly value you is not love at all. True love is found in God, and it is more than enough to sustain us.

Reflection Questions

1. Reflect on a time when you sought validation from people who couldn't give it. How did that experience shape your view of yourself and your worth?
2. Where has God shown His care and love in your life, even when others failed you?
3. How can you begin to shift your focus from seeking validation from others to accepting God's unwavering love for you?
4. What steps can you take to surround yourself with people and environments that reflect God's love for you?

Closing Scriptures:

"Therefore we do not lose heart. Though outwardly we are wasting away, yet inwardly we are being renewed day by day." ---*2 Corinthians 4:16 (NIV)*

"For we are God's workmanship, created in Christ Jesus to do good works, which God prepared in advance for us to do." ---*Ephesians 2:10 (NIV)*

Section 2:

Navigating Personal Challenges with Faith

"In faith there is enough light for those who want to believe and enough shadows to blind those who don't." - *Blaise Pascal*

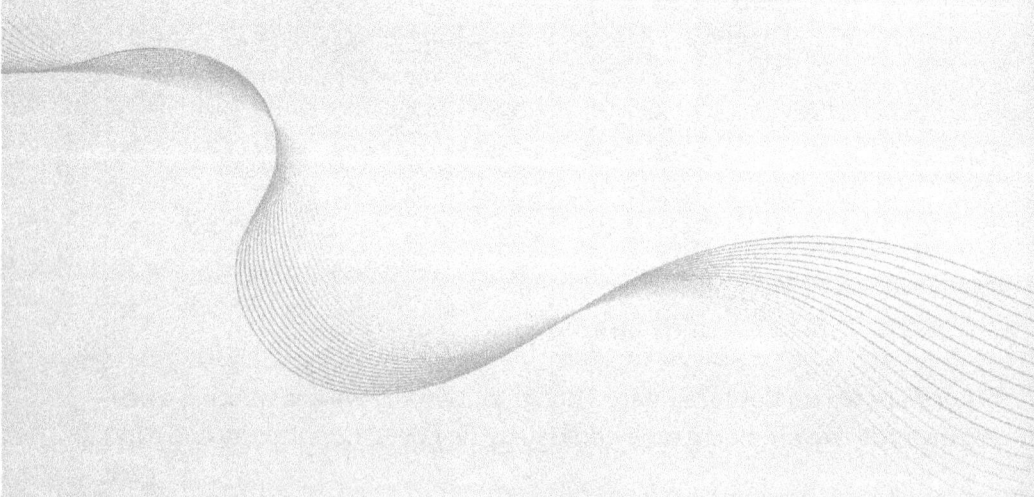

Chapter 6

Finding Joy in the Valley
Embracing God's Peace Amid Hardship

"Daughter, your faith has healed you. Go in peace and be freed from your suffering." ---*Mark 5:34 (NIV)*

"Peace I leave with you; my peace I give you. I do not give to you as the world gives. Do not let your hearts be troubled and do not be afraid." ---*John 14:27 (NIV)*

The Valley of Trials

There are seasons in life that feel like an unending descent into darkness. For me, one of the hardest seasons came when it seemed like every aspect of my life was unraveling at once. Financial pressures loomed like storm clouds, relationships became strained and distant, and a deep loneliness took root in my heart. It was the kind of loneliness that made me feel invisible, even when I was surrounded by people.

Each morning, I would wake up with the faint hope that the day might be different. But as the challenges persisted, that hope began to wane. I felt trapped in an emotional wilderness, unsure of how to move forward. The weight of discouragement grew heavier, and the light at the end of the tunnel seemed farther and farther away.

In those moments of despair, I found myself asking the hard questions: Why is this happening? Where is God in all of this? Does He see what I'm going through? My prayers felt like they were bouncing off the ceiling, and doubt began to creep in, whispering lies that maybe God had forgotten me.

Finding Comfort in God's Presence

One particularly difficult day, I opened my Bible and stumbled across Psalm 23:4: "Even though I walk through the valley of the shadow of death, I will fear no evil, for you are with me; your rod and your staff, they comfort me" (NIV). Those words struck a chord deep within me. I realized that the valley didn't mean God was absent---it was an invitation to draw closer to Him.

That verse became a lifeline. I repeated it to myself daily, letting its truth sink into my heart. God's presence wasn't dependent on my feelings; it was constant, unshakable, and faithful. Another verse that brought me comfort was Isaiah 43:2: "When you pass through the waters, I will be with you; and when you pass through the rivers, they will not sweep over you. When you walk through the fire, you will not be burned; the flames will not set you ablaze" (NIV).

These scriptures reminded me that my struggles weren't evidence of God's absence. Instead, they were opportunities for His presence to shine even brighter. Slowly, I began to see the valley not as a place of despair but as a place of transformation, where God was refining me and teaching me to trust Him in deeper ways.

Joy in the Midst of Pain

One of the hardest lessons I had to learn during this season was that joy and sorrow can coexist. For so long, I thought that joy required the absence of pain, that it was only possible when life was easy and everything was going well. But God showed me that true joy is not dependent on circumstances---it is rooted in Him.

Philippians 4:12-13 became a guiding light for me: "I know what it is to be in need, and I know what it is to have plenty. I have learned the secret of being content in any and every situation, whether well fed or hungry, whether living in plenty or in want. I can do everything through him who gives me strength" (NIV). Like the apostle Paul, I began to see that joy was not about ignoring my pain or pretending it didn't exist. Instead, it was about trusting in God's faithfulness and choosing to see His hand at work, even in the smallest details of my life.

There were still days when the weight of my struggles felt overwhelming, but I began to look for glimpses of God's presence---small moments of peace, an encouraging word from a friend, the beauty of a sunrise. These moments reminded me that God was with me, and they give me the strength to keep going.

The Refining Process

As I reflected on this season, I was reminded of Isaiah 48:10: "See, I have refined you, though not as silver; I have tested you in the furnace of affliction" (NIV). These words captured exactly what I was experiencing. God was using the trials in my life to refine me, stripping away the things I had been relying on for security and teaching me to depend fully on Him.

At first, it was uncomfortable---painful, even. But as I leaned into the process, I began to see the beauty in it. Each hardship was shaping my character, deepening my faith, and strengthening my trust in God. Romans 5:3-4 became a source of encouragement: "Not only so, but we also rejoice in our sufferings, because we know that suffering produces perseverance; perseverance, character; and character, hope" (NIV).

This verse reminded me that my trials were not meant to break me---they were meant to build me up. They were opportunities for God to show His faithfulness, to grow my perseverance, and to remind me that my hope was not in my circumstances but in Him.

God's Faithfulness in the Valley

As I look back on that season now, I can see how God used the valley to draw me closer to Him. James 4:8 says, "Come near to God and he will come near to you" (NIV). That verse became a reality for me. As I turned to God in prayer and reflection, I experienced His presence in ways I never had before.

Even in the darkest moments, He was there, guiding me, comforting me, and strengthening me. His faithfulness became the foundation of my joy---a joy that was not dependent on my circumstances but on the unchanging truth of who He is.

The Call to Move Forward God's Perfect Peace

The valley taught me many lessons, but the most important one was this: God doesn't intend for us to stay in the valley forever. It's a place of refinement and growth, but it's also a stepping stone to something greater. To move forward, I committed to several steps, each rooted in scripture and designed to keep me anchored in God's peace and joy.

1. Daily Time in God's Word and Prayer

I committed to spending intentional time in God's Word and praying every day. Psalm 119:105 says, "Your word is a lamp to my feet and a light for my path" (NIV). This daily practice became a source of strength and guidance, helping me stay connected to God's presence and promises.

2. Practicing Gratitude in All Circumstances

I made it a habit to look for reasons to be grateful, even in the midst of trials. 1 Thessalonians 5:18 reminds us to "give thanks in all circumstances, for this is God's will for you in Christ Jesus" (NIV). Gratitude shifted my perspective from my struggles to God's faithfulness, helping me to see His blessings even in the small things.

3. Connecting with a Supportive Faith Community

I sought out a community of believers who could support me through prayer and encouragement. Ecclesiastes 4:9-10 says, "Two are better than one, because they have a good return for their work: If one falls down, his friend can help him up" (NIV). Through fellowship, I was reminded that I wasn't alone in my journey and that God often uses others to strengthen and uplift us.

4. Meditating on God's Faithfulness

I regularly reflected on the ways God had been faithful in my life. Lamentations 3:22-23 declares, "Because of the Lord's great love we are not consumed, for his compassions never fail. They are new every morning; great is your faithfulness" (NIV). By remembering His goodness, I found the courage to trust Him with my future.

5. Encouraging Others to Seek God's Presence

As I grew in understanding the joy I found in God's presence, I felt called to share it with others. Philippians 4:4 says, "Rejoice in the Lord always. I will say it again: Rejoice!" (NIV). By sharing my story, I hoped to inspire others to lean into God's presence and find their own joy, even in the valleys.

Living with Resilient Joy

To cultivate a resilient joy, I hold onto the truth of Nehemiah 8:10: "Do not grieve, for the joy of the Lord is your strength" (NIV). This joy is neither fleeting nor is it dependent on my circumstances. It is a deep well of strength, empowering me to face life's challenges with courage and faith.

Chapter 7

Wrestling with Myself
Inner Struggles and Spiritual Growth

"Consider it pure joy, my brothers, whenever you face trials of many kinds, because you know that the testing of your faith develops perseverance. Perseverance must finish its work so that you may be mature and complete, not lacking anything." ---*James 1:2-4 (NIV)*

"But those who hope in the Lord will renew their strength. They will soar on wings like eagles; they will run and not grow weary, they will walk and not be faint." ---*Isaiah 40:31 (NIV)*

"Come to me, all you who are weary and burdened, and I will give you rest." ---*Matthew 11:28 (NIV)*

"But he said to me, 'My grace is sufficient for you, for my power is made perfect in weakness.' Therefore I will boast all the more gladly about my weaknesses, so that Christ's power may rest on me." ---*2 Corinthians 12:9 (NIV)*

Living in Silence

Growing up in Sierra Leone, I quickly learned that silence was a survival skill. In our culture, children were expected to observe, not speak, especially about sensitive or emotional matters. Vulnerability wasn't encouraged; it was often misunderstood as weakness. I learned early on to internalize my struggles and shield my emotions from the world.

This unspoken rule shaped my childhood and taught me to rely solely on myself for answers, comfort, and support. I kept my fears, questions, and pain hidden, convinced that speaking up wouldn't change anything. Over time, silence became my way of coping, a shield I used to protect myself from rejection and misunderstanding.

But this habit of silence came with a cost. By keeping my struggles to myself, I unknowingly built walls that isolated me from meaningful relationships. I created imaginary worlds in my mind where I felt loved, seen, and supported. These stories became my escape, offering me temporary relief but preventing me from addressing my true feelings or connecting with others.

London Bridge

Recently, during a family trip to London, the silence I had carried for years finally reached a breaking point. As we walked through the busy streets, I felt an old, familiar ache creeping in. Even though I was surrounded by loved ones, I felt completely alone.

That day, we visited the iconic London Bridge. My family chatted, laughed, and took photos, but I stood on the sidelines, quietly observing. I waited, hoping for someone to notice me, to pull me into the moment and remind me that I mattered. But no one did.

As I stood there, the weight of years of silence and suppression came crashing down. Tears blurred my vision, and I broke down. My family was bewildered, unsure how to respond. They asked what was wrong, urging me to explain. But how could I summarize years of loneliness, of feeling unseen and unheard, into a single sentence?

That moment on London Bridge forced me to confront a painful truth: silence had not been my strength---it had been my prison. By keeping my struggles hidden, I had cut myself off from the very connections I craved. I realized I couldn't continue carrying this burden alone. Something needed to change.

The Cost of Silence

Looking back, I see how silence became both my comfort and my prison. Growing up in a culture that valued emotional restraint, I internalized the belief that sharing my feelings was risky and that being "seen" was a privilege reserved for others.

My family's inability to understand my inner world only reinforced these beliefs. I felt that I had to earn my worth by conforming to others' expectations, suppressing my feelings, and never asking for more than what was given. This belief followed me for years, shaping how I approached relationships and even how I viewed myself.

Silence became my way of coping, but it also robbed me of the love and connection I so deeply desired. By hiding the messier parts of myself, I lost touch with the parts of me that needed love and acceptance the most.

The breakdown on London Bridge was a wake-up call. It forced me to confront the truth I had long ignored: silence wasn't protecting me---it was deepening my wounds. God never asked me to hide my struggles or to pretend I had it all together. Instead, He invites me to bring my burdens to Him, to trust that He loves me as I am, with all my scars and through all my struggles.

A New Understanding of Strength

Through prayer and reflection, I began to see that true strength is not about suppressing emotions or carrying burdens alone. Strength comes from being honest---with myself, with God, and with others.

Psalm 34:18 says, "The Lord is close to the brokenhearted and saves those who are crushed in spirit" (NIV). This verse reminded me that God's love is not conditional on my ability to "hold it together." He draws near in my moments of weakness, offering comfort and peace.

I also found hope in Matthew 11:28-30: "Come to me, all you who are weary and burdened, and I will give you rest. Take my yoke upon you and learn from me, for I am gentle and humble in heart, and you will find rest for your souls. For my yoke is easy and my burden is light" (NIV). These words resonated deeply, reminding me that I didn't have to carry the weight of silence alone. God was inviting me to rest in His presence, to release my burdens, and to trust that His love is sufficient.

Embracing Peace and Authenticity

Through this journey of self-discovery, my desired result is to live with a sense of peace and self-acceptance rooted in God's unconditional love. Psalm 139:14 affirms, "I praise you because I am fearfully and wonderfully made; your works are wonderful, I know that full well" (NIV). This verse has become a cornerstone of my healing, reminding me that my value is not tied to perfection or to meeting others' expectations.

I want to embrace the invitation in 2 Corinthians 12:9: "But he said to me, 'My grace is sufficient for you, for my power is made perfect in weakness.' Therefore I will boast all the more gladly about my weaknesses, so that Christ's power may rest on me" (NIV). By surrendering my weaknesses to God, I am learning to rely on His strength rather than my own. This realization is teaching me to live authentically, free from the need to hide or suppress my true self.

Ultimately, my prayer is to embody the courage to break my silence, trusting that God's love is greater than my fears. I want to live with the confidence that I am fully known and fully loved by Him.

The Call to Move Forward in Nurturing a Relationship with God

Moving forward, I am committing to practices that nurture honesty, self-acceptance, and a deeper relationship with God. These steps are designed to help me break free from silence and embrace the peace that comes from living authentically in His presence.

1. Daily Reflection and Prayer

Each day, I will spend intentional time in prayer, bringing my emotions to God without filter or judgment. Psalm 139:23-24 will guide me: "Search me, O God, and know my heart; test me and know my anxious thoughts. See if there is any offensive way in me, and lead me in the way everlasting" (NIV). In these moments, I will allow myself to simply rest in God's presence, trusting that He accepts me fully.

2. Journaling My Emotions and Faith Journey

I will keep a journal to pour out my thoughts, struggles, and victories. Writing allows me to process my feelings and track my progress, creating a tangible record of God's faithfulness. By documenting my journey, I can see how His grace is working in my life, even in the small steps forward.

3. Building a Support System

I will reach out to trusted friends, mentors, or a faith community where I can share my experiences openly. Ecclesiastes 4:9-10 reminds me: "Two are better than one, because they have a good return for their work: If one falls down, his friend can help him up. But pity the man who falls and has no one to help him up!" (NIV). Through fellowship, I will find encouragement and accountability as I continue to grow.

4. Affirming My Self-Worth

Whenever I feel the pull of self-doubt, I will meditate on scriptures such as 1 Peter 2:9, which declares, "But you are a chosen people, a royal priesthood, a holy nation, a people belonging to God, that you may declare the praises of him who called you out of darkness into his wonderful light" (NIV). Speaking these truths over my life will remind me of my inherent worth in God's eyes, helping me resist the seductive powers of lies of unworthiness.

5. Stepping Out of My Comfort Zone

I will intentionally step into situations or spaces where I can practice vulnerability. Whether it's in sharing my feelings with loved ones or speaking up in moments where I'd typically stay silent, I will trust God to be my strength. Each step forward is an act of faith, a declaration that I am no longer bound by silence.

Living Authentically in God's Love

As I take these five steps, my goal is to live authentically, embracing the peace that comes from resting in God's love. His grace is sufficient, and His power is made perfect in my weakness. By trusting Him with my whole heart, I am finding the courage to break the silence and walk in the fullness of His joy and peace.

Chapter 8

Wrestling with Others
Cultivating Peace and Understanding in Relationships

"Although the Lord gives you the bread of adversity and the water of affliction, your teachers will be hidden no more; with your own eyes you will see them. Whether you turn to the right or to the left, your ears will hear a voice behind you, saying, 'This is the way; walk in it.'"
---*Isaiah 30:20-21 (NIV)*

"Do not be overcome by evil, but overcome evil with good."
---*Romans 12:21 (NIV)*

Balancing Peace and Authenticity

Family relationships can be both a source of comfort and a place of profound challenge. For as long as I can remember, my relationship with my family has been a delicate balancing act. Growing up, I believed that maintaining peace meant avoiding confrontation. I learned to silence my thoughts and feelings, choosing quiet compliance over the risk of upsetting others.

In my culture, speaking up---especially as a young woman---was often discouraged. The prevailing belief was that respect meant staying silent, particularly when it came to emotional matters. To maintain harmony, I learned to bury my hurts, swallowing my needs in the process.

This habit followed me into adulthood, shaping how I navigated conflict and connection within my family. While we shared many moments of joy, there was always an undercurrent of emotional distance. I often felt like an outsider looking in, craving connection but unsure how to bridge the gap.

London Bridge Take 2

As mentioned earlier, during a recent family trip to London, some long-buried tensions came to the surface. The trip, meant to be an opportunity to reconnect and create memories, instead highlighted the unresolved pain I had carried for years.

One evening, after a full day of exploring the city, my family gathered to take photos. As they laughed and posed together, I found myself standing apart, both physically and emotionally. My presence felt incidental, as though I were an observer rather than a participant in my own family.

The next day, while visiting London Bridge, a seemingly minor incident pushed me to my breaking point. My niece asked her mother to take a photo of her, overlooking me entirely. I stood there, waiting for her to ask if I'd like to be in a photo too, but the moment never came. Though it was a small oversight, it felt monumental to me, a painful reminder of the many times I had felt invisible within my family.

The hurt swelled inside me, and I fought to keep it contained. But the weight of years of feeling unseen became too much to bear. Tears began to blur my vision, and for the first time, I allowed myself to express the pain I had long suppressed.

My family, puzzled by my reaction, began to question me. "What's wrong?" they asked, their confusion genuine. But how could I explain the accumulation of emotional wounds that had built up over years? My mother, sensing my distress, tried to console me. Yet her words---intended to soothe---only deepened the hurt. She reminded me of past failures, unintentionally reinforcing the feelings of inadequacy I was struggling to articulate.

Choosing Vulnerability

In that moment on London Bridge, I was faced with a choice: continue the cycle of silence or allow myself to be vulnerable. For the first time, I chose to let my guard down. My tears, my anger, and my pain poured out in their rawest form, unfiltered and undeniable.

It wasn't an easy moment. My family didn't know how to respond to this sudden openness, and I could see their discomfort. But for me, it was a breakthrough. In choosing vulnerability, I understood something I had overlooked for years: peace would not come from staying quiet. True peace required honesty, even if it disrupted the fragile balance of our relationships.

Redefining Peace

Reflecting on this experience, I began to see the patterns of emotional distance that had defined my family relationships. Growing up in an environment where feelings were rarely discussed and conflict was often avoided, I believed that voicing my needs would lead to rejection. I thought that peace meant sacrificing my desires and staying silent, but this approach only fueled feelings of isolation and resentment.

The incident on London Bridge forced me to confront an uncomfortable truth: peace is not simply the absence of conflict. It is a state of mutual understanding and respect, one that requires vulnerability and honesty. For years, I thought staying silent was a way to show respect for my family, but I've come to realize that true respect also includes honoring my own needs and emotions.

Through prayer and reflection, God has shown me that genuine peace requires courage---the courage to express myself, to set boundaries, and to navigate conflict with love. He is teaching me that vulnerability is not a weakness but a doorway to deeper connection. By choosing to share my true self, I am no longer relying on others' approval to feel secure. Instead, I am anchoring myself in God's unwavering love, trusting that His acceptance is the foundation of my worth.

Peace and Understanding

In my relationships, my desired result is to cultivate a peace that honors both myself and others. Ephesians 4:15 challenges me to "speak the truth in love" (NIV). This verse inspires me to approach my relationships with honesty and grace, trusting that God will guide my words to build bridges rather than walls.

Romans 12:18 encourages me: "If it is possible, as far as it depends on you, live at peace with everyone" (NIV). This verse reminds me that peace requires effort and intentionality. It is not about avoiding conflict but about addressing it in a way that fosters understanding and reconciliation.

Colossians 3:13 has also been an inspiration: "Bear with each other and forgive whatever grievances you may have against one another. Forgive as the Lord forgave you" (NIV). This verse reminds me that forgiveness is not about erasing past hurts but about allowing God to transform them into opportunities for growth. By extending grace to myself and others, I can open my heart to the peace and understanding that only God can provide.

Finally, Isaiah 26:3 offers a powerful promise: "You will keep in perfect peace him whose mind is steadfast, because he trusts in you" (NIV). This verse reassures me that true peace is not dependent on my circumstances or others' approval. It is rooted in God's presence, a peace that transcends understanding and equips me to navigate the complexities of human relationships.

The Call to Move Forward in Cultivating Healthy Relationships

As I move forward, I am committing to practices that will help me cultivate peace and understanding in my relationships. These steps are designed to foster honesty, compassion, and respect for both myself and others.

1. Communicating with Intentionality and Kindness

Ephesians 4:15 encourages me to "speak the truth in love" (NIV). I will practice sharing my thoughts openly but with a heart focused on reconciliation rather than blame. Before difficult conversations, I will take time to pray, asking God for wisdom and courage to communicate with grace and empathy.

2. Setting Healthy Boundaries

Romans 12:18 reminds me to focus on what I can control. In pursuit of genuine peace, I will establish boundaries that honor my needs and protect my emotional well-being. Boundaries are a way to nurture healthier relationships, creating space for mutual respect and understanding.

3. Extending Grace and Practicing Forgiveness

Colossians 3:13 calls me to forgive as God forgives. I will seek to release bitterness by surrendering my hurts to Him, trusting that forgiveness is a pathway to healing. Forgiveness doesn't mean tolerating harmful behavior, but it allows me to move forward without the weight of resentment.

4. Praying for Patience and Wisdom

Philippians 4:6-7 reminds me: "Do not be anxious about anything, but in everything, by prayer and petition, with thanksgiving, present your requests to God. And the peace of God, which transcends all understanding, will guard your hearts and your minds in Christ Jesus" (NIV). I will regularly ask God for patience and discernment in my relationships, seeking His guidance to navigate challenges with empathy and understanding.

5. Creating Moments of Connection

To strengthen my relationships, I will intentionally create opportunities for meaningful connection. Whether it's spending time together, sharing experiences, or engaging in honest conversations, these moments will help deepen trust and build stronger bonds.

Living in God's Peace

Isaiah 30:21 reminds me that God's voice will guide me, saying, "This is the way; walk in it." By following His lead, I am learning to cultivate relationships that reflect His love and grace. True peace is not the absence of conflict but the presence of God, equipping me to navigate the complexities of human connection with courage and compassion.

Section 3:

Empowerment and Resilience

"Happiness can be found even in the darkest of times as long as one remembers to turn on the light."
- Albus Dumbledore of the Harry Potter series.

Chapter 9

Self-Advocacy
Becoming Your Own Best Advocate

"It is for freedom that Christ has set us free. Stand firm, then, and do not let yourselves be burdened again by a yoke of slavery."
---*Galatians 5:1 (NIV)*

"I know what it is to be in need, and I know what it is to have plenty. I have learned the secret of being content in any and every situation, whether well fed or hungry, whether living in plenty or in want. I can do everything through him who gives me strength." ---*Philippians 4:12-13 (NIV)*

Silence and Self-Neglect

Throughout much of my life, I was taught---whether directly or indirectly---that advocating for my own needs was selfish. In my family and culture, humility and self-sacrifice were celebrated as virtues. Speaking up for myself, especially as a woman, often seemed like crossing a line, as though voicing my needs might disrupt the harmony around me.

I learned to stay in the background, to put others' needs before my own, and to maintain peace by keeping quiet. If I faced a struggle, I handled it on my own. If I had a need, I waited, hoping someone would notice without me having to ask. Over time, this approach became a way of life---a deeply ingrained pattern that shaped how I interacted with the world and even with myself.

As the years passed, I began to see the cost of this silence. In my relationships, at work, and even in my personal growth, I constantly deferred to others. I told myself that being patient and accommodating would eventually bring the peace and recognition I desired. But instead of feeling fulfilled, I quietly grew frustrated.

My needs were not being met---not because others didn't care, but because I hadn't allowed myself to speak up.

Advocating for My Health

This internal struggle came to a head during a season of health challenges. For months, I felt increasingly unwell, but I hesitated to fully voice my concerns. I didn't want to come across as demanding or "high-maintenance." When I described my symptoms to doctors or family members, I often downplayed their severity, hoping they would connect the dots and take action on my behalf.

As my health continued to decline, I realized that my approach was failing me. My silence was not protecting me---it was costing me my well-being. If I wanted answers and support, I had to step forward and advocate for myself.

At first, the idea of asserting myself felt unnatural, even intimidating. But I knew I couldn't continue on the same path. Slowly, I began taking small steps toward self-advocacy. I started scheduling my own appointments, preparing questions for doctors, and asking for second opinions when I wasn't satisfied with the answers I received.

Each step felt like a challenge, but it also brought a sense of empowerment. For the first time, I began to see my voice as a tool for change---not just for others, but for myself.

The Spiritual Journey of Self-Advocacy

Looking back, I see how much my reluctance to speak up was rooted in cultural expectations and misplaced beliefs about humility. I had convinced myself that staying quiet was a virtue, that being "easy" or "low-maintenance" made me more likable. But over time, I realized that this approach was not true humility---it was a form of self-neglect.

The Bible reminds us that we are "fearfully and wonderfully made" (Psalm 139:14, NIV). This truth challenges me to see my life as valuable in God's sight. Self-advocacy is not about putting myself above others; it is about honoring the life God has given me. When I neglect my needs or remain silent about my struggles, I am failing to steward the gifts He has entrusted to me.

I find comfort in Jesus' interactions in the Gospels, where He consistently showed respect for each person's voice and agency. One moment that stands out is when Jesus asked the man at the pool of Bethesda, "Do you want to get well?" (John 5:6, NIV). In this simple question, Jesus demonstrated a profound respect for the man's desires and choices. This story reminds me that God values my voice and invites me to speak up for my own well-being.

Another powerful example comes from the parable of the persistent widow in Luke 18:1-8. This widow's resilience in seeking justice reflects her belief in her worth and her right to be heard. Her persistence was not selfish---it was an act of faith and determination. This story encourages me to keep advocating for myself, even when it feels challenging or uncomfortable.

Redefining Strength and Humility

Embracing self-advocacy has taught me that it is not about selfishness or pride---it is about living fully and authentically. Galatians 5:1 declares, "It is for freedom that Christ has set us free" (NIV). This verse reminds me that God desires for me to live without the chains of fear or self-doubt.

I have also been inspired by Ephesians 2:10, which says, "For we are God's workmanship, created in Christ Jesus to do good works, which God prepared in advance for us to do" (NIV). This verse challenges me to see self-advocacy as an act of stewardship, a way of honoring the purpose God has placed in my life. By speaking up for myself, I am ensuring that I am healthy, whole, and ready to fulfill the calling He has given me.

True humility, I've learned, is not about shrinking to make

others comfortable. It is about standing confidently in the worth God has given me and trusting that He has equipped me to live boldly.

A Life of Boldness and Peace

My desired result is to live with a deep sense of self-worth, rooted in God's love and purpose. I want to embody the freedom described in Galatians 5:1, trusting that I can advocate for myself without fear.

I also aim to grow in resilience and boldness, as encouraged in Hebrews 4:16: "Let us then approach the throne of grace with confidence, so that we may receive mercy and find grace to help us in our time of need" (NIV). This verse reminds me that I can bring my needs to God with confidence---and that same confidence can extend to my interactions with others.

Lastly, I am inspired by Proverbs 31:25, which says, "She is clothed with strength and dignity; she can laugh at the days to come" (NIV). This verse challenges me to live with courage and joy, seeing my voice as a gift rather than a burden.

The Call to Move Forward in Self-Advocacy

To fully embrace self-advocacy and live in alignment with God's purpose, I am committing to these actionable steps:

1. Speaking with Clarity and Compassion

Proverbs 31:26 says, "She speaks with wisdom, and faithful instruction is on her tongue" (NIV). I will practice speaking openly about my needs, trusting that my voice carries value. This includes approaching conversations with honesty and compassion, knowing that self-advocacy is a reflection of God's love for me.

2. Seeking Knowledge and Support

James 1:5 reminds me, "If any of you lacks wisdom, he should ask God, who gives generously to all without finding fault, and it will be given to him" (NIV). I will seek knowledge and resources in areas where I need support, trusting that God equips those who seek Him. This step includes asking for help, researching solutions, and building a network of encouragement.

3. Setting Boundaries with Confidence

Proverbs 4:23 advises, "Above all else, guard your heart, for it is the wellspring of life" (NIV). I will set boundaries that protect my emotional and spiritual well-being, ensuring that I am living with integrity and purpose.

4. Affirming My God-Given Worth

Isaiah 43:4 declares, "Since you are precious and honored in my sight, and because I love you, I will give men in exchange for you, and people in exchange for your life" (NIV). I will regularly affirm my worth in God's eyes, rejecting the lies of my inadequacy and embracing the truth of His love.

5. Advocating for Others

Hebrews 10:24-25 says, "And let us consider how we may spur one another on toward love and good deeds. Let us not give up meeting together, as some are in the habit of doing, but let us encourage one another—and all the more as you see the Day approaching" (NIV). As I grow in self-advocacy, I will extend this encouragement to others, creating a community of support and empowerment.

Living Boldly in God's Freedom

Isaiah 41:10 reassures me: "So do not fear, for I am with you; do not be dismayed, for I am your God. I will strengthen you and help you; I will uphold you with my righteous right hand" (NIV). By trusting in God's presence, I can stride forward with courage, knowing that He upholds me in every step of this journey.

Chapter 10

Voices of Strength
Knowing and Believing in Your Worth

"And the God of all grace, who called you to his eternal glory in Christ, after you have suffered a little while, will himself restore you and make you strong, firm and steadfast." ---*1 Peter 5:10 (NIV)*

"The light shines in the darkness, but the darkness has not understood it." ---*John 1:5 (NIV)*

"If you falter in times of trouble, how small is your strength!" ---*Proverbs 24:10 (NIV)*

Seeking Worth in the Wrong Places

Growing up, I rarely heard words of affirmation or encouragement. My family placed greater emphasis on achievement and maintaining appearances than on nurturing a deep sense of inner worth. I quickly learned to equate my value with how well I performed, how little space I took up, and how compliant I could be. Over time, I internalized the belief that to be worthy, I had to "earn" love through sacrifice and service to others, often at the expense of my own needs.

This mentality followed me into adulthood, shaping how I approached relationships, work, and personal growth. I became caught in a relentless cycle of striving, constantly seeking validation. I thought that if I could just accomplish enough---at work, in friendships, or even in small, everyday tasks---I would finally feel worthy.

But each achievement felt fleeting. Compliments and praise provided momentary relief, but the sense of inadequacy always returned. It was as though I was trying to fill a bottomless well, pouring in accomplishments and approval but never reaching true fulfillment.

Finding My Anchor in God's Word

This internal struggle came to a head during a particularly challenging season. I was navigating strained relationships, work pressures, and an overwhelming sense of being unseen and unappreciated. Late one night, I found myself crying out to God, desperate for reassurance. In that moment of vulnerability, I opened my Bible and came across Psalm 139:13-14:

> "For you created my inmost being; you knit me together in my mother's womb. I praise you because I am fearfully and wonderfully made; your works are wonderful, I know that full well." (NIV)

These words pierced through my feelings of inadequacy. For the first time, I began to see that my worth was not something I had to earn---it was inherent, woven into my very being by a loving Creator. I realized that my value was not determined by my accomplishments, others' opinions, or even my own self-doubt. It was a truth that existed independently of my circumstances, anchored in God's intentional design.

This revelation was like a light shining in the darkness of my self-doubt. Slowly, I began to internalize the truth that God's love for me was unconditional. It didn't hinge on my performance or my ability to meet others' expectations. In His eyes, I was already valuable, already beloved, just as I was.

From Fragility to Resilience

As I reflect on this journey, I see how easy it is to fall into the trap of measuring our worth by external factors. Society often reinforces the idea that our value comes from what we achieve, how we look, or how we compare to others. But scripture offers a radically different perspective: our worth is intrinsic, rooted in our identity as children of God.

Isaiah 43:4 declares, "Since you are precious and honored in my sight, and because I love you, I will give men in exchange for you, and people in exchange for your life" (NIV). These words have become a source of support for me, a constant reminder that my worth is not something I can gain or lose---it is a reality anchored in God's unchanging love.

Through this process, I've come to understand that my worth is neither fragile nor fleeting. It is resilient, grounded in God's eternal promises. Romans 8:38-39 further solidifies this truth: "For I am convinced that neither death nor life, neither angels nor demons, neither the present nor the future, nor any powers, neither height nor depth, nor anything else in all creation, will be able to separate us from the love of God that is in Christ Jesus our Lord" (NIV). This love is the foundation of my worth, a love that remains steadfast regardless of circumstances, achievements, or failures.

The Woman at the Well: A Reflection of God's Grace

One of the biblical stories that deeply resonates with me is that of the woman at the well in John 4. Jesus approached her with compassion, seeing beyond her past and her circumstances. He recognized her need for living water---a deeper, soul-level fulfillment that no earthly relationship or accomplishment could provide.

In her encounter with Jesus, I see a reflection of my own journey. For so long, I sought validation in external sources, hoping to fill the emptiness I felt inside. But just as Jesus offered the woman at the well the gift of His living water, He offers me the same---a love and worth that are not dependent on my past, my performance, or others' approval.

Walking in Confidence and Purpose

My desired result is to live fully in the confidence of my God-given worth, free from the need to seek validation from external sources. Psalm 139:14 declares that I am "fearfully and wonderfully made," and I want to carry this truth with me in every area of my life.

I also want to embody the boldness described in 2 Timothy 1:7: "For God did not give us a spirit of timidity, but a spirit of power, of love and of self-discipline" (NIV). Living in the reality of my worth means replacing self-doubt with resilience and strength, trusting that God has equipped me to navigate life's challenges with confidence.

Proverbs 31:25 further inspires me to live with dignity and grace: "She is clothed with strength and dignity; she can laugh at the days to come" (NIV). This verse paints a picture of a woman who is not defined by her circumstances but by her unwavering trust in God.

Lastly, I want to extend this understanding of worth to others. Galatians 5:13 reminds us: "You, my brothers, were called to be free. But do not use your freedom to indulge the sinful nature; rather, serve one another in love" (NIV). By affirming my own worth, I can help others recognize theirs, creating a ripple effect of encouragement and empowerment in my community.

The Call to Move Forward in God-given Confidence

To embrace my God-given worth and live in the confidence of His love, I am committing to these practical actions:

1. Daily Affirmations of God's Love and Truth

Each day, I will meditate on verses that affirm my worth, such as Psalm 139:14 and Isaiah 43:4. These scriptures will serve as a shield against negative self-talk and societal pressures, reminding me of my identity as a beloved child of God. Proverbs 4:23 encourages me to "guard [my] heart, for it is the wellspring of life" (NIV), emphasizing the importance of filling my mind with God's truth.

2. Journaling God's Faithfulness and Blessings

I will document moments of gratitude and God's provision in a journal, creating a tangible reminder of His love in my life. 1 Thessalonians 5:18 calls us to "give thanks in all circumstances, for this is God's will for you in Christ Jesus" (NIV). By focusing on God's blessings, I will nurture a spirit of gratitude and reinforce the truth of His unwavering care.

3. Building a Supportive Community

I will surround myself with people who affirm my worth and encourage my growth in Christ. Hebrews 10:24-25 urges us to "consider how we may spur one another on toward love and good deeds. Let us not give up meeting together, as some are in the habit of doing, but let us encourage one another" (NIV). A strong faith community will help me stay grounded in God's truth and provide mutual encouragement.

4. Encouraging Others to See Their Worth

Just as God has revealed my worth to me, I will help others recognize their value. Ephesians 4:29 reminds me: "Do not let any unwholesome talk come out of your mouths, but only what is helpful for building others up according to their needs, that it may benefit those who listen" (NIV). By speaking truth and encouragement into others' lives, I can reflect God's love and create a culture of affirmation.

5. Rejecting Negative Self-Talk and Embracing God's Promises

When negative thoughts arise, I will counter them with God's promises, focusing on verses like Romans 8:38-39, which affirm that nothing can separate me from His love. Romans 12:2 challenges me: "Do not conform any longer to the pattern of this world, but be transformed by the renewing of your mind. Then you will be able to test and approve what God's will is—his good, pleasing and perfect will" (NIV), encouraging me to align my thoughts with God's truth.

Living in the Fullness of God's Love

Colossians 2:10 declares, "and you have been given fullness in Christ, who is the head over every power and authority" (NIV). This verse reminds me that I am already complete in God's eyes. Embracing this truth frees me to live with confidence and purpose, trusting that my worth is secure in His eternal love.

Chapter 11

Joy in Adversity
Discovering Happiness Even When It's Hard

"I consider that our present sufferings are not worth comparing with the glory that will be revealed in us." ---Romans 8:18 (NIV)

"But thanks be to God! He gives us the victory through our Lord Jesus Christ." ---1 Corinthians 15:57 (NIV)

"The Lord is close to the brokenhearted and saves those who are crushed in spirit." ---Psalm 34:18 (NIV)

The Elusiveness of Joy in Hard Times

There have been seasons in my life when joy felt completely out of reach. During these times, life's challenges weighed so heavily that happiness seemed like a distant memory. Joy felt inaccessible, buried beneath layers of pain, worry, and despair.

One particularly difficult season stands out vividly in my memory. Each day seemed to bring a new trial, compounding my burdens and pushing me further into a sense of isolation. I found myself crying out to God, asking why I was enduring so much pain. I desperately wanted to know when, if ever, I would feel joy again.

In one of these moments of vulnerability, I came across Psalm 34:18: "The Lord is close to the brokenhearted and saves those who are crushed in spirit" (NIV). This verse felt like a lifeline, reassuring me that I was not alone in my sorrow. God was near, holding me with a love that refused to let go, even when I felt broken and defeated.

This realization began to shift my perspective. I started to see that my pursuit of joy didn't have to wait for my circumstances to improve. Joy was not something distant or reserved for better days--

-it was something I could begin to experience right where I was, even in the middle of my pain.

Rediscovering Joy in God's Presence

As I reflected on my struggles, I began to notice small but significant moments of joy breaking through the darkness. A kind word from a friend, a passage of scripture that spoke directly to my heart, or the beauty of a quiet sunset would remind me of God's unwavering love. These moments became touchstones, helping me to reconnect with the assurance of His presence.

James 1:2-3 became a guide for me during this time: "Consider it pure joy, my brothers, whenever you face trials of many kinds, because you know that the testing of your faith develops perseverance" (NIV). At first, I struggled to understand how trials could lead to joy. But as I meditated on these words, I began to trust that God was using my challenges to strengthen me, to refine my character, and to draw me closer to Him.

One story that deeply encouraged me during this season was that of Paul and Silas in prison, as recounted in Acts 16:25. Despite their chains and their unjust confinement, they chose to sing hymns and pray, lifting their voices to God in praise. Their example showed me that joy is not dependent on freedom from hardship. Instead, joy is a choice---a deliberate decision to focus on God's faithfulness rather than the pain of the moment.

Over time, I began to understand that joy in adversity does not mean denying my pain. It means acknowledging God's presence within it. Like Paul and Silas, I could choose to praise God even in the darkest places, trusting that His love would sustain me. This realization brought a peace that surpassed all understanding (Philippians 4:7), a peace that became the foundation for a resilient and unshakable joy.

Joy as a Choice and a Gift

Reflecting on my journey, I have come to see that joy is not the absence of struggle---it is the presence of God's peace and love, no matter the circumstances.

In John 16:33, Jesus reassures us: "I have told you these things, so that in me you may have peace. In this world you will have trouble. But take heart! I have overcome the world" (NIV). This powerful truth reminds me that while trials are an inevitable part of life, they do not have the final word. Joy is possible because of the victory we have in Christ, a victory that transcends every difficulty we face.

The call in Philippians 4:4 to "Rejoice in the Lord always. I will say it again: Rejoice!" (NIV) has become central to my understanding of joy. This instruction is not a denial of hardship but an invitation to find joy in God's unchanging love. By shifting my focus from my struggles to His faithfulness, I allow His presence to fill me with peace and hope.

Hebrews 12:2 further inspires me: "Let us fix our eyes on Jesus, the author and perfecter of our faith, who for the joy set before him endured the cross, scorning its shame, and sat down at the right hand of the throne of God" (NIV). Jesus's example reminds me that joy is not about avoiding pain but about finding purpose and strength in God's love.

Living with Resilient Joy

My desired result is to live with a joy that transcends circumstances, grounded in the assurance of God's love and faithfulness. Nehemiah 8:10 declares, "Do not grieve, for the joy of the Lord is your strength" (NIV). This verse reminds me that joy is not fragile or fleeting---it is a source of strength that flows directly from God's heart to mine.

I also want to embody the perspective described in Romans 5:3-5: "Not only so, but we also rejoice in our sufferings, because we know that suffering produces perseverance; perseverance, character; and character, hope. And hope does not disappoint us, because God has poured out his love into our hearts by the Holy Spirit, whom he has given us" (NIV). By allowing my trials to refine me, I can grow in character and hope, trusting that the Holy Spirit will fill me with joy even in adversity.

My goal is to share this joy with others, becoming a source of encouragement and hope. Jesus's words in Matthew 5:16 challenge me: "In the same way, let your light shine before men, that they may see your good deeds and praise your Father in heaven" (NIV). By living with resilient joy, I can inspire others to discover the peace and hope that come from knowing God.

The Call to Move Forward in Joy

To cultivate joy in all seasons, I am committing to these practical steps:

1. Practicing Daily Gratitude

1 Thessalonians 5:16-18 urges us: "Be joyful always; pray continually; give thanks in all circumstances, for this is God's will for you in Christ Jesus" (NIV). I will begin each day by reflecting on God's blessings, both big and small. Gratitude shifts my focus from what I lack to what God has already provided, fostering a spirit of joy and contentment.

2. Seeking God's Presence through Worship and Prayer

Psalm 16:11 reminds me: "You have made known to me the path of life; you will fill me with joy in your presence, with eternal pleasures at your right hand" (NIV). In times of difficulty, I will intentionally seek God through worship and prayer, drawing strength from His peace. Worship allows me to realign my heart with His, finding joy in the reassurance of His constant presence.

3. Meditating on God's Promises

Joshua 1:8 encourages us: "Do not let this Book of the Law depart from your mouth; meditate on it day and night, so that you may be careful to do everything written in it. Then you will be prosperous and successful" (NIV). I will regularly reflect on scriptures that affirm God's faithfulness, allowing His promises to guide my thoughts and sustain my spirit. Verses like Jeremiah 29:11 remind me: "'For I know the plans I have for you,' declares the Lord, 'plans to prosper you and not to harm you, to give you hope and a future'" (NIV), assuring me that God's plans for me are filled with hope and purpose, even when the path feels unclear.

4. Building a Supportive Faith Community

Hebrews 10:24-25 calls us: "And let us consider how we may spur one another on toward love and good deeds. Let us not give up meeting together, as some are in the habit of doing, but let us encourage one another—and all the more as you see the Day approaching" (NIV). I will connect with a community of believers who can provide encouragement and accountability, reminding me of God's faithfulness and helping me cultivate joy.

5. Encouraging Others to Discover Joy in God

Philippians 4:4 calls us to "Rejoice in the Lord always. I will say it again: Rejoice!" (NIV). As I grow in my understanding of joy, I will share this hope with others, offering encouragement to those who feel overwhelmed. By letting God's light shine through me, I can inspire others to find their own joy in Him.

Living in the Victory of Joy

John 15:11 records Jesus's promise: "I have told you this so that my joy may be in you and that your joy may be complete" (NIV). By embracing this joy, I am choosing to live in the victory and hope that God offers, allowing His love to be my strength in every season.

Chapter Notes and Scripture References

Chapter 1: Rediscovering Love -- Healing from Feeling Unloved

1. "I have loved you with an everlasting love; I have drawn you with loving-kindness." -- Jeremiah 31:3 (NIV). This verse reflects God's unchanging love and serves as a reminder that our value comes from Him, not from the approval of others.
2. The "white skirt incident" is a poignant example of the vulnerability that comes from being unprepared for life's changes. It symbolizes how unspoken cultural norms can leave young women feeling isolated and ashamed.
3. The reference to Psalm 34:18 ("The Lord is close to the brokenhearted and saves those who are crushed in spirit" NIV) illustrates how God draws near in times of emotional pain, offering comfort and hope even when others fail us.
4. Journaling and reflection prompts are provided to encourage readers to process their feelings and identify God's presence in their pain. This practice fosters healing and builds faith.

Chapter 2: Embracing Worth -- Conquering Feelings of Insignificance

1. Endometriosis diagnosis and its impact: Endometriosis affects an estimated 10% of women of reproductive age globally, often causing significant pain and emotional strain. The author's experience highlights the importance of advocacy and self-care in navigating chronic health conditions.
2. The story of the woman who touched the hem of Jesus's garment (Matthew 9:20-22) underscores the power of faith to sustain hope, even when physical healing doesn't come immediately or in the way we expect.
3. Psalm 139:13-14 ("For you created my inmost being; you knit me together in my mother's womb. I praise you because I am fearfully and wonderfully made" NIV) serves as a powerful affirmation of self-worth, reminding readers that they are divinely created and deeply loved.
4. Practical steps, such as prayer and educating oneself about health, are emphasized as ways to regain control and combat feelings of helplessness.

Chapter 3: Finding Security -- Overcoming the Fear of Feeling Unsafe

1. The author's memory of being watched while hanging clothes is a relatable depiction of vulnerability and fear. It reflects the universal human need for safety and protection, which God promises in scriptures like Psalm 46:1 ("God is our refuge and strength, an ever-present help in

trouble" NIV).
2. The silence around menstruation in many cultures perpetuates feelings of shame and secrecy, as discussed in the chapter. Normalizing conversations about natural bodily functions can empower young women and build confidence.
3. Proverbs 18:10 ("The name of the Lord is a strong tower; the righteous run to it and are safe" NIV) reminds readers that God provides spiritual refuge even when physical safety feels uncertain.
4. By breaking the silence around her fears and experiences, the author models how vulnerability can lead to healing and how trusting God offers lasting security.

Chapter 4: Recognizing Care -- Transforming the Sense of Being Uncared For

1. Parental absenteeism and its emotional toll: The author's relationship with her father sheds light on how unmet expectations in relationships can lead to feelings of inadequacy and rejection.
2. The reference to 1 Peter 5:7 ("Cast all your anxiety on him because he cares for you" NIV) highlights the importance of trusting in God's constant care, even when human relationships fall short.
3. The inclusion of forgiveness as part of the solution reflects a biblical principle (Matthew 6:14-15) and emphasizes the importance of releasing anger in order to find freedom and healing.
4. Practical steps, such as prayer, reflection, and creating safe spaces for oneself, are woven throughout the chapter to provide actionable ways to heal and recognize God's care.

Chapter 5: Belonging Again -- Healing from Feeling Othered

1. Isaiah 43:2 - "When you pass through the waters, I will be with you; and when you pass through the rivers, they will not sweep over you. When you walk through the fire, you will not be burned; the flames will not set you ablaze" (NIV). Used to emphasize God's presence in trials.
2. Psalm 139:14 - "I praise you because I am fearfully and wonderfully made; your works are wonderful, I know that full well" (NIV). Cited as a cornerstone verse for self-worth.
3. Romans 5:3-4 - "Not only so, but we also rejoice in our sufferings, because we know that suffering produces perseverance; perseverance, character; and character, hope" (NIV). Highlights the transformative power of trials.
4. Matthew 11:28-30 - "Come to me, all you who are weary and burdened, and I will give you rest. Take my yoke upon you and learn from me, for I am gentle and humble in heart, and you will find rest for your souls. For my yoke is easy and my burden is light" (NIV). Points to the rest and renewal found in Jesus during seasons of hardship.
5. Philippians 4:4 - "Rejoice in the Lord always. I will say it again: Rejoice!" (NIV). A call to find joy in God despite life's challenges.

Chapter 6: Joy in the Valley -- Embracing God's Peace Amid Hardship

1. John 14:27 - "Peace I leave with you; my peace I give you. I do not give to you as the world gives. Do not let your hearts be troubled and do not be afraid" (NIV). Anchors the theme of finding peace in God.
2. Psalm 23:4 - "Even though I walk through the valley of the shadow of death, I will fear no evil, for you are with me; your rod and your staff, they comfort me" (NIV). Serves as reassurance of God's presence in trials.
3. Isaiah 48:10 - "See, I have refined you, though not as silver; I have tested you in the furnace of affliction" (NIV). A metaphor for how God uses trials to strengthen faith.
4. Romans 5:3-4 - "Not only so, but we also rejoice in our sufferings, because we know that suffering produces perseverance; perseverance, character; and character, hope" (NIV). Stressed as a reminder of the growth achieved through adversity.
5. Nehemiah 8:10 - "Do not grieve, for the joy of the Lord is your strength" (NIV). The basis for resilient joy rooted in God.
6. James 4:8 - "Come near to God and he will come near to you" (NIV). Encourages readers to seek God actively.
7. Lamentations 3:22-23 - "Because of the Lord's great love we are not consumed, for his compassions never fail. They are new every morning; great is your faithfulness" (NIV). Highlights God's unwavering faithfulness.

Chapter 7: Breaking the Silence -- Finding Peace in Honesty

1. Isaiah 40:31 - "But those who hope in the Lord will renew their strength. They will soar on wings like eagles; they will run and not grow weary, they will walk and not be faint" (NIV). Provides hope and renewal for those carrying burdens.
2. Matthew 11:28-30 - "Come to me, all you who are weary and burdened, and I will give you rest. Take my yoke upon you and learn from me, for I am gentle and humble in heart, and you will find rest for your souls. For my yoke is easy and my burden is light" (NIV). Central to the chapter's call to surrender burdens to God.
3. 2 Corinthians 12:9 - "But he said to me, 'My grace is sufficient for you, for my power is made perfect in weakness.' Therefore I will boast all the more gladly about my weaknesses, so that Christ's power may rest on me" (NIV). Encourages reliance on God's grace in moments of vulnerability.
4. Psalm 34:18 - "The Lord is close to the brokenhearted and saves those who are crushed in spirit" (NIV). Highlights God's care for those in emotional pain.
5. Psalm 139:14 - "I praise you because I am fearfully and wonderfully made; your works are wonderful, I know that full well" (NIV). Reinforces self-worth as rooted in God's design.
6. Philippians 4:6-7 - "Do not be anxious about anything, but in everything, by prayer and petition, with thanksgiving, present your requests to God. And the peace of God, which transcends all understanding, will guard your hearts and your minds in Christ Jesus" (NIV). Connects prayer with

peace that transcends understanding.

Chapter 8: Wrestling with Others -- Cultivating Peace and Understanding in Relationships

1. Isaiah 30:20-21 - "Although the Lord gives you the bread of adversity and the water of affliction, your teachers will be hidden no more; with your own eyes you will see them. Whether you turn to the right or to the left, your ears will hear a voice behind you, saying, 'This is the way; walk in it'" (NIV). Serves as a reminder of God's guidance in relational struggles.
2. Romans 12:21 - "Do not be overcome by evil, but overcome evil with good" (NIV). Offers a call to approach relational challenges with goodness and grace.
3. Ephesians 4:15 - "Instead, speaking the truth in love, we will in all things grow up into him who is the Head, that is, Christ" (NIV). The foundation for honest and compassionate communication.
4. Romans 12:18 - "If it is possible, as far as it depends on you, live at peace with everyone" (NIV). Inspires personal responsibility in seeking reconciliation.
5. Colossians 3:13 - "Bear with each other and forgive whatever grievances you may have against one another. Forgive as the Lord forgave you" (NIV). Highlights the transformative power of forgiveness in relationships.
6. Isaiah 26:3 - "You will keep in perfect peace him whose mind is steadfast, because he trusts in you" (NIV). Grounds peace in the trust of God's presence.
7. Philippians 4:6-7 - "Do not be anxious about anything, but in everything, by prayer and petition, with thanksgiving, present your requests to God. And the peace of God, which transcends all understanding, will guard your hearts and your minds in Christ Jesus" (NIV). Links prayer to emotional and relational peace.

Chapter 9: Self-Advocacy: Becoming Your Own Best Advocate

1. Galatians 5:1 emphasizes the freedom believers have in Christ. This freedom includes the courage to stand firm in our identity and not be burdened by external expectations or societal pressures.
2. Philippians 4:12-13 reflects Paul's resilience, highlighting the source of his strength as Christ. It reminds us that self-advocacy is empowered by God's presence.
3. John 5:6 shows Jesus engaging the man at the pool of Bethesda, emphasizing personal agency in the journey toward healing and well-being.
4. Luke 18:1-8, the parable of the persistent widow, illustrates the importance of perseverance and faith in seeking justice or addressing personal needs.
5. Psalm 139:13-14 reminds us of the divine intentionality in our creation, underscoring the intrinsic value of self-advocacy as honoring God's

handiwork.
6. Proverbs 4:23 underscores the importance of guarding our hearts, which includes setting healthy boundaries as part of self-advocacy.
7. Isaiah 41:10 reassures us that God's strength and presence accompany us in moments of vulnerability, including when we advocate for ourselves.

Chapter 10: Embracing God-Given Worth -- Letting God's Truth Define You

1. John 1:5 speaks to the power of God's light overcoming darkness, symbolizing the enduring truth of our worth in Him.
2. Psalm 139:13-14 serves as a foundational verse, affirming that our worth is woven into our very being by God.
3. Romans 8:38-39 reassures believers of the unshakable nature of God's love, a cornerstone for understanding self-worth.
4. John 4: The story of the woman at the well exemplifies God's ability to see beyond societal labels, affirming our intrinsic value through His grace.
5. Nehemiah 8:10 declares, "Do not grieve, for the joy of the Lord is your strength," reminding us of the connection between joy, worth, and God's faithfulness.
6. Proverbs 31:25 illustrates the dignity and strength found in walking confidently in one's God-given worth.
7. Ephesians 4:29 calls believers to use their words to build others up, reflecting the importance of recognizing and affirming each other's worth in community.

Chapter 11: Joy in Adversity -- Embracing God's Presence Amid Challenges

1. 1 Corinthians 15:57 celebrates the victory believers have in Christ, a reminder that joy is rooted in His eternal truth.
2. Psalm 34:18 highlights God's closeness to the brokenhearted, providing assurance of His presence in difficult seasons.
3. James 1:2-3 encourages believers to find joy in trials, trusting that perseverance and growth will emerge through faith.
4. Acts 16:25 recounts Paul and Silas singing hymns in prison, illustrating the power of choosing joy in adversity.
5. Philippians 4:7 speaks of the peace of God, which surpasses understanding, serving as a foundation for joy amidst challenges.
6. John 16:33 reassures believers of Christ's victory over the world, offering courage and joy even in the face of tribulations.
7. Romans 5:3-5 explains how suffering produces perseverance, character, and hope, linking joy to spiritual growth and resilience.

www.ingramcontent.com/pod-product-compliance
Lightning Source LLC
Chambersburg PA
CBHW032010080426
42735CB00007B/560